What Is the Super Bowl?

by Dina Anastasio

illustrated by David Groff

Grosset & Dunlap
An Imprint of Penguin Random House

For Sue—DA

For my cousin Mike Hurst, the greatest
football fan ever. Go Eagles!—DG

GROSSET & DUNLAP
Penguin Young Readers Group
An Imprint of Penguin Random House LLC

Text copyright © 2015 by Dina Anastasio. Illustrations copyright © 2015 by Penguin Random House LLC. All rights reserved. Published by Grosset & Dunlap, an imprint of Penguin Random House LLC, 345 Hudson Street, New York, New York 10014. Who HQ™ and all related logos are trademarks owned by Penguin Random House LLC. GROSSET & DUNLAP is a trademark of Penguin Random House LLC. Printed in the USA.

Library of Congress Cataloging-in-Publication Data is available.

ISBN 978-0-448-48695-6   10 9 8 7 6

Contents

What Is the Super Bowl?

Some people call it winter's Fourth of July. Others say it's America's biggest party. It happens every year, on a Sunday in January or February. It's *that* Sunday. Super Bowl Sunday.

The Super Bowl is *the* National Football League's championship game. It's the game fans have been thinking about all season.

The Super Bowl is *the* game. It pits the champion of the National Football Conference against the champion of the American Football Conference. No game has more TV viewers. No sports ticket costs more. No other halftime show is louder, brighter, wilder. The winning team takes home a sterling silver trophy. Every winning player receives a gold ring with diamonds. Every team wants to be there. Every fan wants their team to play there.

Super Bowl Sunday finally arrives. Excited fans gather at parties. Bowls of chips and pretzels clutter coffee tables. Millions of people turn on their TVs. Pizzas arrive. Friends and neighbors bring dips and nachos and sandwiches. Restaurants and bars fill up with happy fans.

The luckiest fans head to the stadium where the Super Bowl is being played. There isn't an empty seat anywhere.

The two teams line up across the field from each other. Someone sings "The Star-Spangled Banner." A coin is tossed. One team will kick off and one will receive.

It's time for the kickoff. Eleven players on each team take their positions. Fans in the stadium cheer.

It's starting! fans at home say.

Here we go! fans in restaurants shout.

The kicker kicks the ball. Another Super Bowl begins.

CHAPTER 1
The First Super Bowl

The first Super Bowl was played in Los Angeles on January 15, 1967. The game was called the AFL-NFL World Championship, later known as Super Bowl I.

At halftime, Coach Vince Lombardi was nervous. The score was 14–10. His team, the Green Bay Packers, was four points ahead. But Lombardi knew that four points didn't mean much.

Bart Starr

Everyone had been so sure the Packers would destroy the Kansas City Chiefs. Lombardi's Packers were the National Football League champions. Their quarterback was Bart Starr. He was one of the best players in the league.

The NFL had been around since 1920. They had the experience. NFL teams had the skills. They were stronger and tougher. But Lombardi wondered if this AFL team was better than everybody thought.

The Chiefs were the American Football League champions. They were newcomers. The AFL had started in 1960, forty years after the NFL. The press called them "beginners" and "upstarts."

No one thought the Chiefs had a chance. The nine AFL teams were brash, untamed, messy. Okay, maybe they were good at passing. They might even be faster. But this new league just didn't seem ready.

Kansas City Chiefs

Top tickets at the Los Angeles Coliseum were selling for twelve dollars. In 1967, that price seemed crazy to most people. Who could afford that much for a ticket to a football game? There were empty seats. The game would turn out to be the only Super Bowl in history that wasn't sold out.

Hank Stram

Hank Stram was the coach of the Kansas City Chiefs. He was worried, too. The Chiefs had an excellent defense. But they would have to work harder than ever to stop Bart Starr. This wasn't just a game to determine the best football *team* in America. This was a game to prove the AFL could compete against the big guys.

As Lombardi gave his team a halftime pep talk, jazz musician Al Hirt played his trumpet on the field. Two marching bands performed.

Al Hirt

When the second half began, it looked like the Chiefs had a chance. A four-point lead wasn't enough to guarantee a win.

Len Dawson, the Chiefs' quarterback, tried to throw a pass. The Packers defense went to work. They rushed him. Willie Wood intercepted the pass and ran fifty yards to the Kansas City

five-yard line. Elijah Pitts scored the touchdown. Suddenly the score was Packers 21, Chiefs 10. Vince Lombardi began to breathe easier.

The Packers stepped it up even more. Starr threw one successful pass after another. The game ended. Final score: Packers 35, Chiefs 10.

Green Bay took home the trophy and the winning-team rings. Bart Starr was named the game's Most Valuable Player.

The press reported that the AFL team had been crushed, just as expected. But at least it wasn't a shutout. The AFL needed more time, more experience. Maybe they'd win one . . . someday.

On January 14, 1968, Vince Lombardi's NFL Green Bay Packers traveled to Miami to defend their title. This was the second AFL-NFL World Championship game. It would later be known as Super Bowl II.

WORLD PROFESSIONAL
FOOTBALL CHAMPIONSHIP

U.S. ANGELES MEMORIAL COLISEUM
JANUARY 15, 1967

GREEN BAY PACKERS 35
KANSAS CITY CHIEFS 10

Once again, no one thought the AFL team had a chance. The Oakland Raiders needed practice. People called them another upstart team from an upstart league.

Super Bowl II ended with a final score of Green Bay 33, Oakland 14. The American Football League was dismissed as the little league that couldn't. No AFL team would ever be able to compete against the mighty NFL.

Or would they?

Vince Lombardi

Vince Lombardi was born in Brooklyn, New York, on June 11, 1913. He helped his parents take care of his four younger brothers and sisters. He worked in his father's butcher shop. He played football in his Brooklyn neighborhood. At Fordham University, he was a star on a winning football team. But he was small. Vince decided to take a job as a high-school coach. His St. Cecilia team became the best in the country. In 1959, Lombardi became head coach of the struggling Green Bay Packers. He worked his players hard. Soon the team was winning games. At the end of his first season, Lombardi was named Coach of the Year. The Packers kept winning. They won five NFL championships. Vince Lombardi was one of the greatest NFL coaches ever. When he died in 1970, the World Professional Championship Trophy was renamed in his honor. Each year, the winning Super Bowl team receives the Vince Lombardi Trophy.

CHAPTER 2
The Team That Couldn't

January 9, 1969. It was three days before the third AFL-NFL World Championship game. The NFL's Baltimore Colts were to face the AFL's New York Jets in Miami, Florida.

It seemed like everyone but the Jets thought the Jets would lose. The Colts were favored to win by eighteen points. Joe Namath was the Jets' quarterback. He was sick of hearing they didn't have a chance. He was bored with reading that an American Football League team couldn't win a Super Bowl.

Namath's nickname was "Joe Cool" for a reason. Not much bothered him. But on that day somebody made a joke about the Jets, and Joe Cool lost his cool. He made an announcement that nobody ever forgot.

"We're gonna win the game," Namath said. "I guarantee it." He sounded so sure that everyone in the room started to laugh.

Three days later, on January 12, 1969, the Jets met the Colts in Miami for the Super Bowl.

Roman numerals are used to keep track of Super Bowls.							
1	2	3	4	5	6	7	8
I	II	III	IV	V	VI	VII	VIII
9	10	20	30	40	50	60	
IX	X	XX	XXX	XL	L	LX	

Don Shula was the coach of the Baltimore Colts. The Colts' star quarterback was Johnny Unitas. People called him the Golden Arm. Unitas was one of the greatest quarterbacks ever. But he had missed most of the season due to an injury. He still wasn't really fit to play.

Shula had studied the Jets. Joe Namath was walking the confident *I'll show you!* walk. The Jets looked strong. They seemed prepared. Was an upset possible?

No one scored for most of the first half. But then, just before halftime, Namath completed four passes. Then, fullback Matt Snell scored a

Matt Snell

touchdown. Jim Turner's extra-point kick was good. At halftime the score was 7–0.

Hold on here! What was going on? People were starting to wonder if a brash, young upstart AFL team could win a Super Bowl.

The answer turned out to be one of the biggest upsets in the history of the NFL. Jim Turner kicked three field goals for the Jets. The Jets defense kept the Colts offense from scoring until the fourth quarter.

Final score: New York Jets 16, Baltimore Colts 7. Joe Namath was named the game's Most Valuable Player. An AFL team had finally won. The unthinkable had happened.

The next day, one of the most famous football photos of all time appeared in newspapers. The picture showed Namath leaving the field with his index finger raised. One finger meant *We're number one*. Joe Namath had promised a win, and the Jets had delivered.

Joe Namath

Joe Namath was born and raised in Beaver Falls, Pennsylvania. In high school, he played basketball, baseball, and football. He was so good, he was scouted in all three sports. Several major baseball teams wanted him, but Joe's mother insisted he go to college.

The University of Alabama offered Joe a full scholarship to play football. Joe turned in his baseball glove and headed south. His coach was Paul "Bear" Bryant. Bryant later called him "the greatest athlete I ever coached."

On November 28, 1964, Namath was the New York Jets' first pick in the yearly draft. Joe was so excited about his new career in the pros that he quit college before graduation. But forty-two years later, in 2007, he finished college and earned his Alabama degree.

CHAPTER 3
It Takes a Kicker

On January 11, 1970, Hank Stram and his Kansas City Chiefs returned for Super Bowl IV. This time they were there to play the Minnesota

Vikings. Once again, most people expected the AFL Chiefs to lose. They said the Jets' win had just been a fluke.

They were wrong. The Chiefs were out for revenge. They were determined to win this one. The Chiefs led from the start. Quarterback Len Dawson connected on pass after pass. He was named the game MVP. But it was placekicker

Jan Stenerud who scored the first nine points. His first field goal sailed forty-eight yards, a Super Bowl record. For thirty years, it remained the longest Super Bowl field goal ever kicked.

The score was 3–0. Stenerud kicked another. The score was 6–0. He kicked one more. The score was 9–0. Stenerud kicked an extra point after a Chiefs touchdown. Then he kicked one more.

The final score was Kansas City 23, Minnesota 7. The Chiefs' placekicker had scored eleven points. An AFL team had won the Super Bowl for the second time. No one was making jokes about the AFL anymore!

The Kick that Changed the Game

In 1964, Pete Gogolak was a kicker for the Buffalo Bills. All other kickers used their toes to kick. They kicked straight ahead. Pete kicked with the inside of his foot. He placed his field goals perfectly. He rarely missed an extra-point kick. The press wrote stories about his odd way of kicking.

The reason for it was that Pete grew up playing soccer in Hungary. Soccer players kick with the inside of their feet.

Jan Stenerud grew up in Europe, too. He played soccer in Norway. He also kicked with the inside of his foot. Today the soccer-style kick is used by every placekicker in the NFL.

Super Bowl V Baltimore Colts

Super Bowl V was played in Miami, Florida, on January 17, 1971. The Baltimore Colts had lost Super Bowl III. Now they were back. This time they were up against the Dallas Cowboys.

Don McCafferty was the Colts' new head coach. He had coached the offense under Don Shula for eight years. It was his first season, and he had taken the Colts to the Super Bowl.

Super Bowl V turned out to be one of the sloppiest Super Bowl games ever. Some people called it the "Blunder Bowl." Both teams fumbled their way into history. Pass after pass was intercepted. The Colts turned the ball over to the other team seven times. The Cowboys gave the ball up four times. Their record of eleven combined turnovers is still tied for most ever in a Super Bowl.

In the end, the Colts won. But it was not the great victory that the team had hoped for. The final score was 16–13. Chuck Howley was named Super Bowl V's MVP. Howley was a Dallas Cowboys linebacker. He played for the *losing* team! That had never happened before. It has never happened since. Howley thought the defeat made the award meaningless. He refused to accept it.

The Leagues Merge

Super Bowl V was the first game played between the new NFC (National Football Conference) and the AFC (American Football Conference). During the 1970 season, the NFL and the AFL had merged into one NFL league with two conferences. But there was a problem. The AFC had fewer teams than the NFC. Three NFC teams would have to switch over. The Baltimore Colts, the Cleveland Browns, and the Pittsburgh Steelers agreed to join the AFC.

CHAPTER 4
An Almost-Perfect Shutout

In 1970, Don Shula left the Colts to coach the Miami Dolphins. The Dolphins offense consisted of great players like Bob Griese, Larry Csonka, and Larry Little. Under Shula, their running game grew stronger. Shula's defense was becoming unstoppable.

On January 14, 1973, the Dolphins arrived at Super Bowl VII with a perfect record. During the 1972 regular season, the Dolphins won every game. They won all their playoff games. They were undefeated. Their 1972 season record was 16–0–0. Sixteen wins, zero losses, zero ties. If they took the Super Bowl, too, they would become the first NFL team to win all their games. Their record would be 17–0–0. Sports history!

The Dolphins were playing the Washington Redskins in Super Bowl VII. The game was played in Los Angeles, California. It was the hottest day in Super Bowl history: 84 degrees.

The Dolphins scored two touchdowns during the first half. Garo Yepremian added two points with his extra-point kicks. The Dolphins left the field at halftime leading 14–0. They returned for the second half feeling fine.

With a little more than two and a half minutes left in the game, the Redskins still had not scored.

The Miami defense was overwhelming. Even Shula was sure the Dolphins were going to win. Fans were hoping for a final score of 17–0. They wanted the same number as their season record. That would be sweet indeed.

The seconds were ticking away. Shula decided on a field goal. He sent in their placekicker, Yepremian. Garo was an excellent kicker. A three-point kick would mean a 17–0 score.

Garo stepped back. He kicked the ball. It sailed low and was blocked by a Redskins tackle. The ball flew up in the air and bounced. Then things really got crazy. Garo picked it up and began to run. But the Redskins defense was closing in. Garo panicked. He tried to pass. But before he could, the ball slipped out of his hands. Mike Bass grabbed the ball and scored the only Redskins touchdown.

The play was immediately labeled Garo's Gaffe. It is still talked about to this day.

The final score of Super Bowl VII was 14–7. The Dolphins are still the only NFL team to play an entire season undefeated.

Don Shula

There's never been a coach quite like Don Shula. Shula was a head coach for thirty-three years. During his career, he won 347 games. No coach has ever won as many. Shula's teams have made it to a record six Super Bowls. In his second season with the Dolphins, he took his team all the way to Super Bowl VI. The Dolphins lost to the Dallas Cowboys, but Shula had learned a thing or two. The Dolphins won every game the next season. They returned for Super Bowl VII with a perfect record. Shula retired from coaching after the 1995 season.

CHAPTER 5
The Steelers Rule the 1970s

The 1969 season was about to begin. The Steelers had been around for thirty-six years. They had made the playoffs only once, and they had lost. Now they had a new coach, Chuck Noll. Pittsburgh fans were ready to win. They were counting on Noll.

Noll turned out to be a genius at spotting talent. In 1969 he drafted defensive tackle "Mean Joe" Greene. Then, in the early 1970s, he signed Terry

Bradshaw, Jack Ham, Lynn Swann, and several other future Hall of Famers. Noll transformed the defense into a fortress. People were calling them the "Steel Curtain." Before long, Chuck Noll had created a winning machine that ruled the 1970s.

On January 18, 1976, the Pittsburgh Steelers met the Dallas Cowboys in Miami, Florida. They were there for Super Bowl X.

The Steelers and the Cowboys had been rivals for a long time. Both teams had won one Super Bowl. The Cowboys had brought home the Super Bowl VI trophy. The Steelers had won Super Bowl IX the year before. Fans for both teams held pregame parties. Dallas fans wore blue and white shirts. Pittsburgh fans wore black and gold.

Two weeks earlier, Steelers receiver Lynn Swann had been hit hard in a playoff game against the Raiders. The hit had landed him in the hospital with a concussion. Doctors weren't sure if he

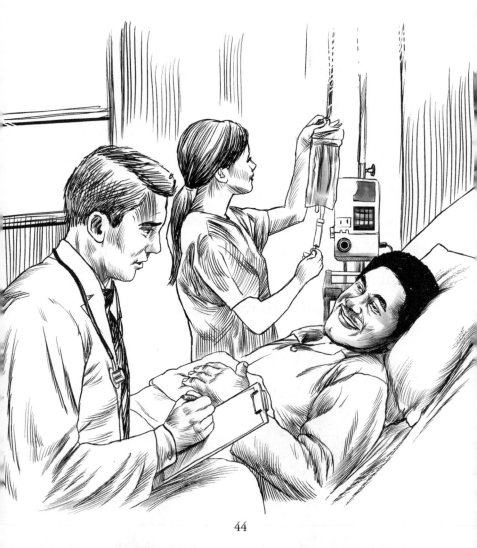

would be able to play in the Super Bowl. Swann wasn't sure, either. Soon the dizziness faded, but Swann was still thinking about whether to play. Then something happened that helped him decide. It was a few days before the game. Cliff Harris, a Dallas player, told the press that "I'm not going to hurt anyone intentionally, but getting hit again while he's on a pass route must be in the back of Swann's mind. I know it would be in the back of my mind."

Swann was angry. He thought Harris was trying to play with his confidence. That decided it! He would play.

Lynn Swann made four soaring catches in Super Bowl X. But there was one catch that everyone still talks about. They call it the Swann Dive. They say it was like watching the ballet *Swan Lake*. It happened at the end of the second quarter. Pittsburgh was behind 10–7. Up in the stands, fans of both teams were going crazy.

The play began with a pass from Pittsburgh quarterback Terry Bradshaw. Swann watched it come. Mark Washington, the Cowboys' cornerback, watched it, too. He was crammed up against Swann, eyes glued to the ball. They moved together as the ball sailed toward them. Steelers fans jumped up and waited. Cowboys fans were on their feet too. *Stop him!* they shouted.

The ball sailed over Washington's head. Washington bounded up and tipped the ball. Swann soared higher. Lunging. Tipping the ball . . . Juggling it. Diving forward. Stretching. Flying forward like a glider. His fingers wrapping the ball. Sliding to the ground.

As the game went on, things turned rough. Roger Staubach, the Cowboys' quarterback, was sacked seven times. Cliff Harris patted the Steelers' kicker Roy Gerela on his helmet. Then he thanked him for "helping" Dallas. Gerela's teammate Jack Lambert evened things up by grabbing Harris and heaving him to the ground. With less than five minutes left in the game, Bradshaw threw a sixty-four-yard pass. Swann caught it. He scored a touchdown. But Bradshaw never saw it happen. As the ball left his hand, Larry Cole, a Dallas lineman, hit him hard. He led with the top of his helmet, like a bull. Bradshaw left the field with a concussion.

The final score was Pittsburgh 21, Dallas 17. Pittsburgh took home the trophy for the second time.

Two years later, Dallas beat the Denver Broncos in Super Bowl XII. The Cowboys-Steelers Super Bowl race was tied. Then, on January 21, 1979, both teams returned to the Miami Orange Bowl for Super Bowl XIII. Pittsburgh won 35–31. Lynn Swann caught seven passes, and Terry Bradshaw was named MVP.

The Steelers finished their 1979 season at Super Bowl XIV. The game was played in the Los Angeles Rose Bowl Stadium, on January 20, 1980. The Los Angeles Rams didn't have a chance. Terry Bradshaw's passes connected. Pittsburgh's "Steel Curtain" defense stopped play after play.

The 1970s were over. The Steelers had won four Super Bowls in six years. Their coach, Chuck Noll, had built one of the greatest teams that ever played football. He had created a dynasty.

In the early 1980s, many of Pittsburgh's star players retired. By 1984, Joe Greene, Lynn Swann, and Terry Bradshaw were gone. The Steelers didn't return to the Super Bowl for twenty-six years.

Keeping It Safe

In 2013, the NFL decided something had to be done about safety. Terry Bradshaw and other players had developed serious brain injuries. It happened from their heads getting pounded for years. Now they couldn't remember things. Defensive players talked about all the concussions they had suffered. A new rule was passed. Hitting with the crown of a helmet would no longer be allowed. Players would receive a fifteen-yard penalty.

CHAPTER 6
49ers or Bust

Another NFL dynasty ruled the 1980s. In 1979, a new coach joined the San Francisco 49ers. Bill Walsh understood that a great team begins with great talent and a winning plan.

Walsh immediately drafted quarterback Joe Montana and wide receiver Dwight Clark. Then he went to work developing one of the greatest passing games football has ever seen. Walsh believed that short passes were the best offense. They were hard to keep up with. They fooled the other team's defense.

Bill Walsh

In 1981, the Niners made the playoffs. During the last minute of the game against the Dallas Cowboys, "The Catch" happened. It remains one of football's most famous plays. Clark was in the end zone. Montana passed the ball. The ball sailed too high. It was almost out of bounds. Clark flew up. His fingers grasped for the ball. And then he had it. Touchdown!

The 49ers were on their way to the Super Bowl.

Two weeks later, on January 24, 1982, the 49ers played the Cincinnati Bengals in Super Bowl XVI. It was the first Super Bowl game for both teams. It was the the first time a Super Bowl game was played in a cold city. The temperature in Pontiac, Michigan, was below freezing. But inside the Superdome, it was a warm 72 degrees.

Diana Ross sang "The Star-Spangled Banner," and the game began. Eighty-five million people were watching on TV. Niners fans cheered for Joe Montana, although many viewers had never heard of the young quarterback before this game. Now they sat up and took notice of

Joe Montana

his perfectly timed, perfectly placed short and middle passes. The Niners won 26–21. Montana was named MVP.

Three years later, on January 20, 1985, the Niners returned for their second Super Bowl win. Once again, Joe Montana was the MVP.

Bill Walsh continued to draft great players. In 1985, Walsh drafted one of the best players of all—Jerry Rice. Jerry Rice was an awesome wide receiver. No one could catch Montana's passes like Jerry Rice.

Jerry Rice

Then, on January 22, 1989, the team played in Super Bowl XXIII in Miami. They faced the Cincinnati Bengals. In that game, Walsh's players came together for one of the most exciting drives in football history.

The game was almost over. There were only about three minutes left. San Francisco was behind. The score was 16–13. San Francisco needed to move the ball ninety-two yards, or they were going to lose.

Joe Montana had played and won two Super Bowls before, in 1982 and 1985. Jerry Rice had watched those games. He had studied Montana. He had wondered what it would be like to receive passes from him. Now it was really happening.

Montana stepped back. He raised his arm. He looked around. He let the ball go. It sailed into the arms of Roger Craig. He threw another pass. John Frank caught it. Then a pass to Rice. Another to Rice. One more to Craig.

The ball was on the forty-five-yard line. The clock was clicking down. A little more than one minute to go.

Super Bowl XXIII San Francisco 49ers

Montana passed to Rice. Rice caught it and ran. The Bengals defense couldn't stop him until he reached the eighteen-yard line.

The clock read thirty-nine seconds left. Montana passed the ball to Craig. On the final play, the Bengals were all over Rice. Montana looked for another receiver. John Taylor was in the end zone. Montana threw the ball. Taylor caught it.

Final score: San Francisco 20, Cincinnati 16. The 49ers had pulled it out. Jerry Rice had caught eleven passes for 215 yards. He was named the Super Bowl MVP.

On January 28, 1990, the 49ers were back for Super Bowl XXIV. The Niners met the Denver Broncos in the New Orleans Superdome and ended their super decade with a fourth Super Bowl win.

Coach Bill Walsh had retired after Super Bowl XXIII. But most of his players remained. Joe Montana was still the quarterback. Jerry Rice was still catching Montana's passes and racing toward the end zone.

The 49ers didn't just win Super Bowl XXIV. They destroyed the Broncos. They broke records. The final score was 55–10. No team has ever scored that many points in a Super Bowl before. The point difference is still the largest in any Super Bowl. Joe Montana earned the game MVP

award for the third time. No other player had ever
won that many.

The 49ers had tied the Pittsburgh Steelers'
record for most Super Bowl wins in a decade. The
Steelers had won four during the 1970s. Now the
49ers had won four in the 1980s.

CHAPTER 7
Here Come the Cowboys

The 1980s were not a great decade for the Dallas Cowboys. In the 1970s, the team had won the Super Bowl twice. But throughout the eighties, they hadn't managed to grab the trophy once. Meanwhile, their rivals in the NFC, the 49ers, had won four Super Bowls.

Then, in 1989, a new coach took over for the Cowboys, and things began to change. Jimmy Johnson brought in new talent. He created new plays. The plays worked. Fans noticed. Maybe the Cowboys weren't such a bad team after all.

In 1990 and 1991, the Cowboys got better and better. And in 1992, it all came together for the team. On January 31, 1993, Dallas played the Buffalo Bills in Super Bowl XXVII.

The game took place at the Rose Bowl in Pasadena, California. One hundred and thirty-three million people in the United States watched on TV. Country superstar Garth Brooks sang the national anthem.

At halftime, the score was 28–10 for the Cowboys. The teams left the field, and the biggest halftime show ever began. Michael Jackson seemed to shoot out of a video. He reappeared on a stage at the fifty-yard line. He froze. The crowd roared. He didn't move. The crowd waited. They waited some more. The show began with a part of the song "Jam." The crowd jumped up and started dancing along with Michael to "Billie Jean" and "Black or White." Other Jackson hits followed. The show ended with thousands of Los Angeles children singing along to "Heal the World." Fireworks lit up the sky.

For the first time, more people watched the halftime show than the game. The Super Bowl would never be the same again. From then on, big names rocked halftime shows: Janet Jackson, the Rolling Stones, Beyoncé, Bruce Springsteen, Madonna, U2, Prince.

The Cowboys won Super Bowl XXVII. Final score: Dallas 52, Bills 17. Everyone agreed they were a great team again. But how great?

The Cowboys had three Super Bowl wins. The 49ers and the Steelers were tied with four. If the Cowboys could win one more, they'd be in a three-way tie.

A year later, on January 30, 1994, the Cowboys won the NFC and returned for Super Bowl XXVIII. Once again, they played the Bills. Once again, they won. Final score: Dallas 30, Bills 13.

The Cowboys had tied the record: Steelers: four; 49ers: four; Cowboys: four.

Fans all over America were taking sides during the 1994 season. Who would play in the next Super Bowl? Would one of these three teams win it and break the tie? Two weeks before Super Bowl XXIX, the Cowboys and the 49ers battled it out for the NFC championship. On the same day, the Pittsburgh Steelers played the San Diego Chargers for the AFC title.

By nightfall it was decided. The 49ers were heading to Miami to meet the Chargers in Super Bowl XXIX. If the 49ers won, they would break the three-way tie.

On Super Bowl Sunday, January 29, 1995, it took the Niners less than two minutes to show the world they were in it to win it. Steve Young had replaced Joe Montana as the Niners' quarterback. At one minute and forty-four seconds, Jerry Rice caught a pass from Young and scored touchdown number one.

The final score was 49–26. The Niners had won their fifth Super Bowl.

The 1995 season was another battle of the dynasties. The 49ers were determined to hang on to their record. The Steelers were out to tie it. But no one was as hungry for the trophy as the Cowboys.

The Cowboys managed to win the NFC championship. Now they had their chance. If they could win Super Bowl XXX, they'd tie the Niners for the most Super Bowl wins.

But there was one problem. The Steelers had won the AFC championship. Dallas would be playing Pittsburgh in Super Bowl XXX. The Steelers wanted that win, bad. But the Dallas team wanted it more.

On January 28, 1996, the Cowboys met the Steelers in Tempe, Arizona. Dallas took an early lead and held on to it till the game ended. The Steelers fought hard, but Dallas brought home the trophy. Final score: Dallas 27, Pittsburgh 17.

The Cowboys were now tied for the record: 49ers: five; Cowboys: five; Steelers: four.

The rivalry between these three teams has never let up. Ten years later, the Steelers beat the Seattle Seahawks in Super Bowl XL and tied

the 49ers for most wins: five to five. Then, three years after that, they beat the Arizona Cardinals in Super Bowl XLIII.

The Steelers had won six Super Bowls. The Cowboys and the 49ers had both won five. As of 2014, the Steelers still held the record.

CHAPTER 8
Almost Overtime

If a pro football game ends in a tie, it goes into overtime.

No Super Bowl game has ever gone into overtime. But some have come very close.

It was January 30, 2000. The St. Louis Rams were playing the Tennessee Titans in Atlanta, Georgia. Both teams arrived at Super Bowl XXXIV with 13–3 season records.

St. Louis was ahead 9–0 at halftime. Most people thought they would win. The Titans tied the game, 16–16, in the second half, but the Rams scored again, retaking the lead. At six seconds left in the game, St. Louis was ahead by seven points. The score was St. Louis 23, Tennessee Titans 16. The Titans needed a touchdown to tie the game. A tie would send the game into overtime.

The Titans had used up all their time-outs. They were on the ten-yard line. There was time for one more play. Ten yards to the end zone for six points. Then one good extra-point kick to tie the score.

Titans quarterback Steve McNair stepped back. He was ready to throw a pass to Kevin Dyson. But a Rams linebacker named Mike Jones saw it coming. He saw it in Dyson's eyes before the ball was in the air.

The clock was counting down. Jones took off. McNair threw the ball. Four seconds. Dyson caught it on the five-yard line and turned. He headed for the end zone.

Mike Jones was almost on him. There were two seconds left. Jones grabbed Dyson's leg and hung on. Dyson fell to the ground, inches from the goal line. He stretched out his arm. One second. Not enough. He stretched it farther. Still not enough.

The game was over. Final score Rams 23, Titans 16.

They called the play "The Tackle." It was one of the best defensive plays, bar none. Everyone who was there remembers it. They still talk about it. *The Tackle?* they say. *I'll never forget it. It was the most exciting thing I've ever seen.*

Vince Lombardi teaches strategy to the Green Bay Packers, 1963

Los Angeles Memorial Coliseum, home of Super Bowl I

Max McGee scores for the Green Bay Packers in Super Bowl I

Green Bay Packers' Bart Starr picks up a first down in Super Bowl II

Baltimore Colts' Johnny Unitas in Super Bowl V

Dallas Cowboys' Chuck Howley intercepts a pass in Super Bowl VI

The Pittsburgh Steelers' "Steel Curtain" in Super Bowl IX

New York Giants' Pete Gogolak kicks a field goal

San Francisco 49ers' Dwight Clark catches a pass in Super Bowl XVI

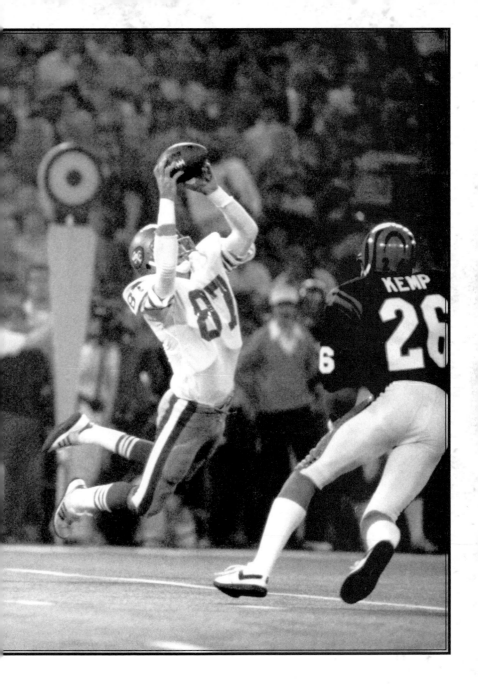

San Francisco 49ers' Jerry Rice dives into the end zone in Super Bowl XXIII

"The Tackle" – Tennessee Titans' Kevin Dyson reaches for the end zone as St. Louis Rams' Mike Jones wrestles him to the ground in Super Bowl XXXIV

Dallas Cowboys' Tony Romo throws a pass

Fans wear team colors to cheer on their favorite players

Green Bay Packers' Donald Driver jumps into the crowd after a touchdown

New England Patriots' Tom Brady celebrates at a victory parade

Bruno Mars performs during halftime at Super Bowl XLVIII

Joe Namath at Super Bowl XLVIII

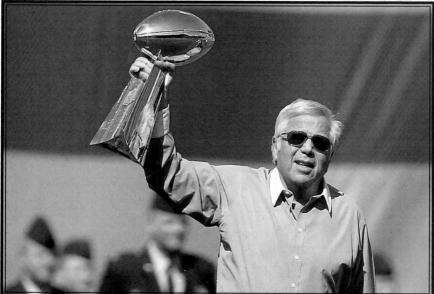

New England Patriots owner Robert Kraft holds
the Vince Lombardi Trophy on April 13, 2015

Soldier Field, NFL's oldest stadium and home of the Chicago Bears

Two years later, in the New Orleans Superdome, the New England Patriots' Adam Vinatieri made a kick that sailed into history. There were less than five seconds left in Super Bowl XXXVI. The score was tied: Patriots 17, St. Louis Rams 17. The Patriots had a choice. They could hold the ball until time ran out. The score would stay at 17–17. This meant overtime. Or they could try to win with a three-point field goal. If the kick was good, they could win it now.

Adam Vinatieri was a great kicker. He was so good that everyone called him Automatic Adam. Adam trotted onto the field to kick the field goal. This would be the final play of the game.

Adam stepped back. He kicked. The ball sailed forty-eight yards. The ref raised his arms. The field goal was good. Adam had broken the tie. The Patriots had won. Final score: 20–17.

Two years after that, in Super Bowl XXXVIII, Automatic Adam did it again. It was February 1, 2004. The Patriots were playing the Carolina Panthers. Once again, it looked like the game was going into overtime. Once again, there were less than five seconds left in the game. The score was tied: Patriots 29, Panthers 29.

Adam stepped up. He kicked. The ball sailed toward the goalposts. He raised his arms. He knew the kick was good. He felt it when his foot touched the ball. His perfect kick sailed forty-one yards. The Patriots had won again. Final score: Patriots 32, Panthers 29.

CHAPTER 9
Super Brothers

Super Bowl XLII: February 3, 2008

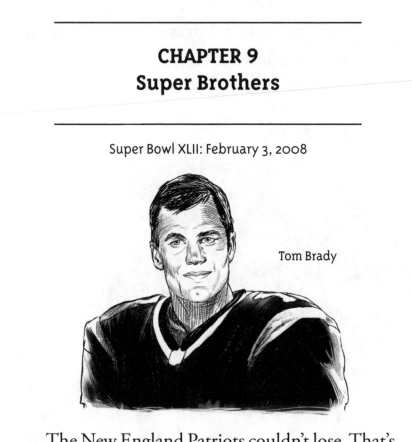

Tom Brady

The New England Patriots couldn't lose. That's what everybody was saying. The AFC champions hadn't lost a game all season. Tom Brady was one of the greatest quarterbacks anyone had ever seen. He'd been named the Super Bowl MVP twice, in 2002 and 2004.

Most people thought the New York Giants weren't ready. Okay, Eli Manning was a good quarterback, but he was young. He'd never beat Tom Brady. And Eli would never live up to what his brother had done.

Eli's big brother Peyton had won the Super Bowl MVP the year before. The press had twice voted him the league's most valuable player. Eli was proud of his brother. But it was hard when people said he'd never be as good.

At the start of the game, everyone thought Brady and the Patriots would win big. But by halftime, people were having second thoughts. The Patriots were leading, but only by four points. The score was 7–3. Giants fans in Arizona's University of Phoenix stadium were cheering louder. Patriots fans were getting worried.

The score stayed 7–3 until the fourth quarter. Then Eli threw a forty-five-yard pass. The Giants were moving closer to the end zone. Eli completed

another pass. Touchdown! Giants fans jumped to
their feet. Their roar echoed through the stadium.
Giants 10, Patriots 7. It was amazing! It was
staggering! The Giants were leading.

　　With less than three minutes left, the Patriots
scored. The score was Tom Brady and the Patriots
14, Eli Manning and the Giants 10.

And then it happened. The Giants started working their way down the field. Eli completed pass after pass. The din in the stadium was deafening.

Giants fans were standing, shaking their fists, urging their team on. Fans at home were screaming at their TVs. Eli hurled the ball. It sailed thirty-two yards. David Tyree leaped into the air and grabbed it. He held it against his helmet until he was tackled. People call it the "Helmet Catch," and it was one of the most amazing catches ever made.

Final score: Giants 17, Patriots 14. Some people say it was the greatest upset in NFL history. Eli Manning was named the game's MVP. His big brother Peyton had won it the year before, and now it was Eli's turn.

Eli and Peyton went into the record books. They have both won a Super Bowl MVP award. No other brothers have done that.

Growing Up Manning

Peyton and Eli Manning grew up in a football family. Their father, Archie, played professional football when they were young. Their older brother Cooper played in college.

The Manning brothers played ball with Archie when they were growing up in New Orleans, Louisiana. Archie played quarterback. Peyton and

Eli liked throwing the ball, too. That meant Cooper had a lot of passes to receive.

Cooper and Peyton were football stars in high school. Cooper was a winning wide receiver. Peyton was the star quarterback. Eli was younger. He went to their games with his parents. He watched and learned.

Peyton and Eli went on to become professional star quarterbacks. Their parents came to many of their games. Cooper came, too. Back problems had ended Cooper's own chance at a career in pro football. Still, he is proud of his brothers and cheers them on. He was there for Super Bowl XLVI in 2012 when Eli was named MVP the second time. And he was there when Peyton played in Super Bowl XLVIII on February 2, 2014.

No brothers, players or coaches, ever played against each other in a Super Bowl until the "Harbaugh Bowl."

Jim and John Harbaugh were two of the best coaches in the NFL. They were also brothers. On February 3, 2013, they met in the New Orleans Superdome for Super Bowl XLVII. Jim Harbaugh was the coach of the San Francisco 49ers. John Harbaugh coached the Baltimore Ravens. Some people called it the "Blackout Bowl," because the Superdome lost its power for more than half an hour. But others called it the "Harbaugh Bowl" or the "Brother Bowl."

John Harbaugh's Ravens led for the whole game. As the game wound down, it looked like the 49ers had a chance to win. However, the final score was Ravens 34, 49ers 31.

When the game was over, John Harbaugh was a jumble of mixed-up emotions. On the one hand, he was thrilled about winning. But he also felt sad that his little brother had lost. He was filled with pride and admiration for Jim and the job he had done. "He's the best coach in football right now," John said. "Anybody out there who has a brother can understand what that is all about."

CHAPTER 10
How Do You Stop a Legend?

On February 2, 2014, the Seattle Seahawks played the Denver Broncos in Super Bowl XLVIII. The Seattle Seahawks were young. Their average age was 26.4 years old. Russell Wilson was the Seahawks' quarterback. Wilson was only twenty-five. He'd been playing in the NFL for two seasons. This was his first Super Bowl.

Everyone knew he was smart. They knew he could pass. But did he have enough experience?

Russell Wilson

Peyton Manning was the Denver Broncos' quarterback. At thirty-seven years old, he was a legend. One of the greatest. He had more NFL MVP awards than any other player in history. He'd played in two Super Bowls. He had won a Super Bowl ring. He was a Super Bowl MVP.

The Broncos' 2013 season had been one for the books. They shattered the record for most points scored in one season, with 606. Manning broke two NFL records: most touchdown passes in a season (fifty-five) and most yards passing.

The Broncos had a great offense, but the Seahawks had something the Broncos didn't. They had the number one defense in the NFL. Their defense had allowed the fewest yards. It had allowed the fewest points. Each team had finished the season with a 13–3 record. Could the team with the best defense beat the team with the best offense?

The game was held in MetLife stadium in East Rutherford, New Jersey. Before this, no Super

Bowl had been played in an open stadium in a cold-weather state. A few days before, the weather had been freezing. But it was warmer now.

Joe Namath tossed the coin at the start of the game. Seattle won the toss and chose to receive.

The Broncos lined up. The Broncos' center crouched. He snapped the ball back to Peyton. The ball flew over Peyton's head and landed in the Seahawks' end zone. The Broncos' running back got to the ball before the Seahawks. But the Seahawks brought him down before he could scramble out.

"Safety!" the ref called. When a player causes the ball to be "dead" in the other team's end zone, a "safety" is called and his team is awarded two points. Seattle was ahead 2–0. The game had only begun twelve seconds earlier. No team had ever scored so soon in a Super Bowl.

Seattle scored two field goals and a touchdown. The score was 15–0. Manning threw a pass. Linebacker Malcolm Smith saw it coming

and intercepted. He kept running—all the way to the Broncos' end zone. Touchdown! The score at halftime: Seahawks 22, Broncos 0.

It was looking bad for the Broncos, and it only got worse. After the Broncos kicked off the second half, the Seahawks scored another touchdown. The score was Seahawks 29, Broncos 0.

The Seahawks defensive backfield was living up to its nickname: "the Legion of Boom." They were on fire. They knocked a Manning pass away. Seattle got the ball. Seattle scored again: 36–0.

The third quarter was winding down. Manning was able to complete pass after pass, and the Broncos finally scored. They went for a two-point conversion. The score: Seahawks 36, Broncos 8.

The Seahawks scored another touchdown at eleven minutes left in the game. The Legion of Boom wouldn't quit. They stopped almost every play the Broncos tried. Final score: Seahawks 43, Broncos 8. The young Seahawks were the NFL champions.

On February 1, 2015, the Seattle Seahawks returned for Super Bowl XLIX. For the second year in a row, they faced a legend. The New England Patriots and their star quarterback, Tom Brady, had played in six Super Bowls, winning three. Brady had won Super Bowl MVP twice before.

The forty-ninth Super Bowl was held at University of Phoenix Stadium, in Glendale, Arizona. Once again, Seattle's Legion of Boom was ready. Once again, they were the best defense in the league. They had stopped Peyton Manning the year before, and this year they were determined to hold off Tom Brady. But as the game progressed, two of Seattle's best defensive players couldn't play due to injuries.

Again and again, Tom Brady's passes connected. With twenty seconds left in the game, the score was Patriots 28, Seahawks 24. But Seattle had the ball on the one-yard line. They only needed one yard to score the winning touchdown!

Most people assumed Seattle would let their star running back, Marshawn Lynch, push his way past the goal line, but Seattle's coach, Pete Carroll, called for a pass. Russell Wilson threw the ball. Malcolm Butler, a rookie Patriots defensive back, was there. He intercepted the ball in the end zone. The Seahawks lost. Final score: Patriots 28, Seahawks 24.

Tom Brady was named the game's MVP, tying Joe Montana's record of three Super Bowl MVP trophies.

Tom Brady

Many things had changed since the Green Bay Packers won the first Super Bowl in 1967. There were new rules. Helmets were tougher. Coaches called different plays. More fans gathered to cheer on their teams. The cost of a ticket had skyrocketed. In 1967, the top ticket was $12. By 2015, many fans were paying one thousand times that much.

In 1967, high school and college bands marched at halftime. In 2014, the audience became part of the biggest video show ever. As the Red Hot Chili Peppers and Bruno Mars performed, eighty thousand hats lit up. There were three LEDs and a small receiver in each one. In 2015, Katy Perry rode into the stadium on a huge mechanical lion. She ended her show by flying away on a shooting-star platform.

Still, much has stayed the same. The two best teams compete for the championship. A coin toss starts the game. Coaches still call the plays. Quarterbacks throw passes. Receivers leap into the sky and catch them. Everyone tries to score a touchdown. Fans cheer for their teams. The winning team takes home a sterling silver trophy with a silver football on top. Championship rings are still presented. A Most Valuable Player is chosen.

People talk about how the Super Bowl has changed. But has it? Not really.

Tuning In for the Ads

Not only do viewers get excited to watch the game, they also enjoy seeing the commercials. Over the years, some of the most memorable TV ads have aired during the Super Bowl.

In 1975, a McDonald's ad showed people of all ages trying to sing the "You Deserve a Break Today" song. In 1980, a famous ad starred "Mean Joe" Greene. After a game, a kid offers Greene a Coke. Joe takes it and—returning the favor—tosses the kid his football jersey. Apple introduced the first Mac computer in 1984 in a Super Bowl commercial.

Of course, airing an ad during the Super Bowl doesn't come cheap. In 2013, a thirty-second ad that showed talking babies trading stock tips cost about $3,800,000!

Timeline of the Super Bowl

Super Bowl	Date	Winners	Score	Losers
I	Jan. 15, 1967	Green Bay Packers	35–10	Kansas City Chiefs
II	Jan. 14, 1968	Green Bay Packers	33–14	Oakland Raiders
III	Jan. 12, 1969	New York Jets	16–7	Baltimore Colts
IV	Jan. 11, 1970	Kansas City Chiefs	23–7	Minnesota Vikings
V	Jan. 17, 1971	Baltimore Colts	16–13	Dallas Cowboys
VI	Jan. 16, 1972	Dallas Cowboys	24–3	Miami Dolphins
VII	Jan. 14, 1973	Miami Dolphins	14–7	Washington Redskins
VIII	Jan. 13, 1974	Miami Dolphins	24–7	Minnesota Vikings
IX	Jan. 12, 1975	Pittsburgh Steelers	16–6	Minnesota Vikings
X	Jan. 18, 1976	Pittsburgh Steelers	21–17	Dallas Cowboys
XI	Jan. 9, 1977	Oakland Raiders	32–14	Minnesota Vikings
XII	Jan. 15, 1978	Dallas Cowboys	27–10	Denver Broncos
XIII	Jan. 21, 1979	Pittsburgh Steelers	35–31	Dallas Cowboys
XIV	Jan. 20, 1980	Pittsburgh Steelers	31–19	Los Angeles Rams
XV	Jan. 25, 1981	Oakland Raiders	27–10	Philadelphia Eagles
XVI	Jan. 24, 1982	San Francisco 49ers	26–21	Cincinnati Bengals
XVII	Jan. 30, 1983	Washington Redskins	27–17	Miami Dolphins
XVIII	Jan. 22, 1984	Los Angeles Raiders	38–9	Washington Redskins
XIX	Jan. 20, 1985	San Francisco 49ers	38–16	Miami Dolphins
XX	Jan. 26, 1986	Chicago Bears	46–10	New England Patriots
XXI	Jan. 25, 1987	New York Giants	39–20	Denver Broncos
XXII	Jan. 31, 1988	Washington Redskins	42–10	Denver Broncos
XXIII	Jan. 22, 1989	San Francisco 49ers	20–16	Cincinnati Bengals
XXIV	Jan. 28, 1990	San Francisco 49ers	55–10	Denver Broncos
XXV	Jan. 27, 1991	New York Giants	20–19	Buffalo Bills

Super Bowl	Date	Winners	Score	Losers
XXVI	Jan. 26, 1992	Washington Redskins	37–24	Buffalo Bills
XXVII	Jan. 31, 1993	Dallas Cowboys	52–17	Buffalo Bills
XXVIII	Jan. 30, 1994	Dallas Cowboys	30–13	Buffalo Bills
XXIX	Jan. 29, 1995	San Francisco 49ers	49–26	San Diego Chargers
XXX	Jan. 28, 1996	Dallas Cowboys	27–17	Pittsburgh Steelers
XXXI	Jan. 26, 1997	Green Bay Packers	35–21	New England Patriots
XXXII	Jan. 25, 1998	Denver Broncos	31–24	Green Bay Packers
XXXIII	Jan. 31, 1999	Denver Broncos	34–19	Atlanta Falcons
XXXIV	Jan. 30, 2000	St. Louis Rams	23–16	Tennessee Titans
XXXV	Jan. 28, 2001	Baltimore Ravens	34–7	New York Giants
XXXVI	Feb. 3, 2002	New England Patriots	20–17	St. Louis Rams
XXXVII	Jan. 26, 2003	Tampa Bay Buccaneers	48–21	Oakland Raiders
XXXVIII	Feb. 1, 2004	New England Patriots	32–29	Carolina Panthers
XXXIX	Feb. 6, 2005	New England Patriots	24–21	Philadelphia Eagles
XL	Feb. 5, 2006	Pittsburgh Steelers	21–10	Seattle Seahawks
XLI	Feb. 4, 2007	Indianapolis Colts	29–17	Chicago Bears
XLII	Feb. 3, 2008	New York Giants	17–14	New England Patriots
XLIII	Feb. 1, 2009	Pittsburgh Steelers	27–23	Arizona Cardinals
XLIV	Feb. 7, 2010	New Orleans Saints	31–17	Indianapolis Colts
XLV	Feb. 6, 2011	Green Bay Packers	31–25	Pittsburgh Steelers
XLVI	Feb. 5, 2012	New York Giants	21–17	New England Patriots
XLVII	Feb. 3, 2013	Baltimore Ravens	34–31	San Francisco 49ers
XLVIII	Feb. 2, 2014	Seattle Seahawks	43–8	Denver Broncos
XLIX	Feb. 1, 2015	New England Patriots	28–24	Seattle Seahawks
L	Feb. 7, 2016	Denver Broncos	24–10	Carolina Panthers

Timeline of the World

1967	Thurgood Marshall is sworn in as the first African American justice of the US Supreme Court
1969	Woodstock rock festival is held in upstate New York
	US astronaut Neil Armstrong walks on the moon
1972	Atari releases the first generation of video games with an arcade version of *Pong*
1975	Vietnam War officially ends with the fall of Saigon
	The first International Women's Day is observed by the United Nations
1977	US scientists discover the rings of Uranus
1981	Tohui the Mexican panda becomes the first panda to be born and survive outside of China
1988	A wildfire at Yellowstone National Park brings awareness to global warming
1989	Students protest the Chinese government in Tiananmen Square in Beijing
	The Berlin Wall falls
1990	Sir Tim Berners-Lee invents the World Wide Web
1994	Nelson Mandela is elected the first black president of South Africa
	The Channel Tunnel under the English Channel connects England and France
1996	Dolly the sheep becomes the first cloned mammal
1997	The Harry Potter series by J. K. Rowling debuts

2001	—	Terrorist attacks kill almost three thousand people in the World Trade Center, the Pentagon, and a field in Pennsylvania
2007	—	Usain Bolt runs 100 meters in 9.72 seconds to break the world record
2013	—	Pope Francis becomes the first pope in history from Latin America

Bibliography

*Books for Young Readers

* Der, Bob, ed. *Sports Illustrated Kids Big Book of Who: Football*.
New York: Time Home Entertainment, 2013.

Karpf, Rory. *The Book of Manning*. Directed by Rory Karpf. TV film.
ESPN Films, 2013.

Manning, Peyton, Archie Manning, and John Underwood. *Manning*.
New York: HarperEntertainment, 2000.

McGinn, Bob. *The Ultimate Super Bowl Book: A Complete Reference
to the Stats, Stars, and Stories Behind Football's Biggest Game—
and Why the Best Team Won*. Minneapolis: MVP Books, 2009.

Syken, Bill, ed. *Sports Illustrated Football's Greatest*. New York:
Sports Illustrated Books, 2012.

Websites

ESPN
www.espn.go.com

National Football League
www.nfl.com

Pro Football Hall of Fame
www.profootballhof.com

Pro Football Reference
www.pro-football-
reference.com

Sports Illustrated
www.si.com

Super Bowl History
www.superbowlhistory.net

Vince Lombardi Official Website
www.vincelombardi.com

Glossary

AFC: Short for the American Football Conference. The AFC is one of the two conferences in the National Football League. The other is the National Football Conference. Each conference consists of sixteen teams.

Blitz: When members of the defense try to tackle the opposing quarterback

Chain gang: Six men who use a chain to help measure yards covered

Completion: A pass caught by the same team's receiver

Dynasty: A team that wins many championships during a period of time, often a decade

Extra-man penalty: Called when more than eleven team members are on the field

Extra point: The one-point kick that follows a touchdown

Field goal: A three-point kick. A field goal is good when the ball is kicked through the goalposts, above the bar.

Goal line: The front line of the end zone. A touchdown is scored when the ball goes over the goal line.

Instant replay: Some football plays are too close to call. Officials might use TV replays to review a referee's decision to see if it was correct.

NFC: Short for the National Football Conference. One of the two National Football League conferences. The other is the American Football Conference.

Offside penalty: Called when a player is over the scrimmage line when the ball is snapped

Playbook: A secret book filled with a team's game plans and plays that all players must learn

Punt: A fourth-down kick that results in a change of possession. The punter must drop and kick the ball before it hits the ground.

Safety: A safety is called when a player with the ball is tackled behind his own goal line. It results in two points for the other team.

Shutout: The losing team scores no points

Snap: When the center starts a play by passing the ball back to the quarterback

Time out: This stops the clock. In the Super Bowl, each team is allowed three time-outs.

Two-point conversion: When the offense runs or passes to get into the end zone after a touchdown instead of kicking for an extra point

Zebras: A nickname for the NFL refs, because their black-and-white shirts are striped like zebras